Charlotte Perkins Gilman's

# The Yellow Wallpaper

Peter Leigh

Published in association with The Basic Skills Agency

## Hodder & Stoughton

A MEMBER OF THE HODDER HEADLINE GROUP

**Acknowledgements**
*Cover: Fred Van Deelen*
*Illustrations: Jim Eldridge*
*Photograph of Charlotte Perkins Gilman © The Hulton Getty Picture Collection Limited*

Orders: please contact Bookpoint Ltd, 39 Milton Park, Abingdon, Oxon OX14 4TD. Telephone: (44) 01235 400414, Fax: (44) 01235 400454. Lines are open from 9.00–6.00, Monday to Saturday, with a 24 hour message answering service. Email address: orders@bookpoint.co.uk

*British Library Cataloguing in Publication Data*
A catalogue record for this title is available from The British Library

ISBN 0 340 74308 5

First published 1999
Impression number  10 9 8 7 6 5 4 3 2
Year                        2005 2004 2003 2002 2001 2000 1999

Typeset by Fakenham Photosetting Ltd, Fakenham, Norfolk.
Printed in Great Britain for Hodder & Stoughton Educational, a division of Hodder Headline Plc, 338 Euston Road, London NW1 3BH by Redwood Books, Trowbridge, Wiltshire.

## About the author

Charlotte Perkins Gilman was born in
America in 1860. She was famous both
as a writer and as a fighter for the rights
of women. In 1935 she discovered she
had cancer. She committed suicide.

# About the story

This is a strange story.
Some find it very disturbing,
others find it very sad.

There are only two people in it –
the writer and John, her husband.
They have rented a big house
for the summer.

But that's not what the story is about.
What the story is about
is what it is like to go mad!

# I

It is very seldom
that ordinary people
like John and myself
can rent a grand house like this
for the summer.

It must be that there is
something queer about it.
Else, why should it be let so cheaply?
And why has it stood so long empty?

John laughs at me, of course,
but I expect that.

**practical** –
down to earth

John believes that
if you can't see
something, then it's
not there.

He is very practical.
He is not at all superstitious,
and he laughs at talk of things unseen.

John is a doctor,
and perhaps that is the reason
I do not get well faster.

You see, he does not believe I am sick.
And what can I do?

**respected** –
everyone looks up
to him

**a slight hysterical
tendency** – she
becomes disturbed
easily

If your own husband
is a respected doctor,
and he tells your friends and relatives
that there is really
nothing the matter with you
but nerves –
'a slight hysterical tendency' –
what can you do?

My brother is also a doctor,
also respected,
and he says the same thing.

So I take medicines, and tonics,
the air, and exercise,
and I am told I must not 'work'
until I am well again.

Personally, I don't agree.
Personally, I think that pleasant work,
with excitement and change,
would do me good.
But what can I do?

I did write for a while
in spite of them,
but it does tire me a good deal,
because I have to be so sly about it,
or else face the row.

So I will let it alone
and talk about the house.

It is the most beautiful place.
It is quite alone,
and stands well back from the road.

There is a lovely garden!
I never saw such a garden!
It is large and shady
with paths and seats.
There were greenhouses,
but they are all broken now.

The place has been empty for years.
There is something strange about it –
I can feel it.

I even said so to John
one moonlit evening,
but he said what I felt was a draught,
and shut the window.

He said I mustn't start imagining things,
imagining things is bad for me.
He says I need to control myself.

He is very careful and loving,
and hardly lets me move by myself.

I don't like our room a bit.
I wanted one downstairs
that opened onto the patio,
and had roses all over the window.
But John would not hear of it.

It is a big, airy room.
Some of the paper
has been pulled off –
in great patches
all around the head of my bed,
about as far as I can reach,
and in a great place
on the other side of the room,
low down.

I never saw a worse paper in my life.
An ugly sprawling pattern,
that gives you a headache to look at it.

The colour is repellent,
almost revolting –
a thick, dirty yellow,
dull yet lurid in some places,
sickly and faded in others.

I should hate it,
if I had to live in this room for long.

There comes John,
and I must put this away –
he hates to have me write a word.

**sprawling pattern** –
the wallpaper is a
messy design
**repellent** – make
you sick

**lurid** – too bright

# II

We have been here two weeks,
and I haven't felt like writing before.

I am sitting by the window now,
up in this horrible room.
John is away all day,
and even some nights
when his cases are serious.

I am glad my case is not serious.
But these 'nerves' are so depressing.
I suppose John never had 'nerves'
in his life.
He laughs at me so much
about this wallpaper.

At first he meant to repaper the room.
But then he said
that I was letting it get the better of me,
and that nothing was worse
than letting things get the better of me.
He said that after the wallpaper,
it would be the bed, then the windows,
then the stairs, and so on.

'You know the place
is doing you good,' he said.
'Really, dear,
I don't want to decorate the house,
when we're only here
for three months.'

'Then do let us go downstairs,' I said.
'There are such pretty rooms there.'

Then he took me in his arms,
and called me a blessed little goose.
He said we would
go down to the cellar, if I wished,
and have it whitewashed as well.

He is right.
It's just a whim.
I feel silly.
I'm really getting fond of the big room,
all but that horrid paper.

**whim** – a silly idea

John says that when I get really well,
we will ask Henry and Julia for a visit,
but it would be bad for me
to have those stimulating people
around me now.

**stimulating** –
exciting

I wish I could get well faster.

But I mustn't think about that.

This paper looks as if it knows
what a bad effect it has.
There is a spot where the pattern
looks like two big eyes
staring at you upside down.

As I said before,
it's torn off in spots,
and it's ever so difficult to get off!
And the floor is scratched
and gouged and splintered,
the plaster is dug out here and there,
and this great heavy bed
looks as if it has been bitten.

But I don't mind a bit –
only the paper.

**gouged** – marked

# III

I cry at nothing,
and cry most of the time.

Of course I don't when John is here,
but when I am alone.

And I am alone a good deal just now.
John is kept in town very often
by serious cases.

So I walk a little in the garden,
or sit on the porch under the roses,
or lie down up here.

I'm getting really fond of the room
in spite of the wallpaper.
Perhaps *because* of the wallpaper.

**dwells** – stays

It dwells on my mind so.

I lie here on this great bed,
and follow the pattern about.

I haven't said this to John,
but there are things in that wallpaper.
There are things
that nobody knows about but me,
or ever will.
Behind that pattern
the dim shape gets clearer every day.
It is always the same shape –
like a woman stooping down
and creeping about behind that pattern.

I don't like it a bit.
I wonder –
I begin to think –
I wish John would take me away
from here!

It is so hard to talk with John
about my case,
because he is so wise,
and because he loves me so.
But I tried it last night.

It was moonlight.
The moon shines in all around
just as the sun does.
I hate to see it sometimes,
it creeps so slowly,
and always comes in by one window
or another.

John was asleep,
and I hated to wake him.
So I kept still,
and watched the moonlight
on the wallpaper till I felt creepy.

The faint figure behind
seemed to shake the pattern,
just as if she wanted to get out.

I got up softly,
and went to feel if the paper *did* move,
and when I came back John was awake.

'What is it, little girl?' he said.
'Don't go walking about like that –
you'll catch cold.'

I thought it was a good time to talk,
so I told him that
I was really not getting better here,
and that I wished
he would take me away.

'Why darling,' he said,
'we'll be leaving in three weeks.
We can't leave before.
You really are better, dear,
whether you can see it or not.
I am a doctor, dear, and I know.'

'I'm not better.
Maybe in the evening when you are here,
but not in the morning
when you are away.'

'Bless her little heart,'
said he with a big hug.
'She shall be as sick as she pleases.
But now let's go to sleep,
and talk about it in the morning.'

'And you won't take me away?'
I asked gloomily.

**gloomily** – unhappily

13

'Why, how can I, dear?
It's only three weeks more.
Really, dear, you are better.'

So of course I said no more,
and we went to sleep before long.
He thought I was asleep first,
but I wasn't, and lay there for hours,
looking at the wallpaper.

At night, in any kind of light,
it becomes bars!

The pattern, I mean,
and the woman behind it
as plain as can be.

I didn't see for a long time
what the thing was that showed behind,
but now I am quite sure it is a woman.

By daylight she is quiet.
I think it is the pattern
that keeps her so still.
It is so puzzling.
It keeps me quiet by the hour.

I lie down ever so much now.
John says it is good for me,
and to sleep all I can.

He made me lie down
for an hour after each meal.

But I don't sleep.
I look at the wallpaper!

# IV

Life is very much more exciting now
than it used to be.
You see, I have something
to look forward to,
something to watch.
I really am better,
and am more quiet than I was.

John is so pleased to see me get better.
He laughed the other day,
and said I seemed to be getting better
in spite of my wallpaper.

I laughed,
because I didn't want to tell him
it was *because* of the wallpaper.
He would make fun of me.
He might even want to take me away.

I don't want to leave now
until I have found out
what is in the wallpaper.
There is a week more,
and that will be enough.

I'm feeling so much better!

I don't sleep much at night,
because it is so interesting
to watch the paper.
But I sleep a good deal during the day.

It is the strangest yellow,
that wallpaper!
It makes me think
of all the yellow things I ever saw –
not beautiful ones like buttercups,
but old, foul, bad yellow things.

But there is something else
about that wallpaper – the smell!

I noticed it
the moment we came into the room.
But with so much air and sun,
it was not so bad.

But now it creeps all over the house.

**hovering** –
hanging around
**skulking** – sneaking

I find it hovering in the dining room,
skulking in the parlour,
hiding in the hall,
lying in wait for me on the stairs.

17

It gets into my hair.

Such a strange smell, too!
I have spent hours
trying to work out what it is like.

It is not bad – at first –
but in this damp weather it is awful.
I wake up in the night,
and find it hanging over me.

It used to disturb me.
I wanted to burn the house –
to reach the smell.

But now I am used to it.
I think it is like the *colour*
of the paper!
A yellow smell.

There is a very funny mark
on this wall.
It's low down, near the skirting board.
A streak that runs round the room.
It goes behind every piece of furniture,
except the bed.
A long, straight, even streak,
as if it had been rubbed over and over.

I wonder how it was done,
and who did it,
and what they did it for.
Round and round and round –
round and round and round –
it makes me dizzy.
I really have found something out
at last.
I have found out that the pattern
*does* move – and no wonder!
The woman behind shakes it!

She creeps around fast,
and her creeping shakes it all over.
Then she keeps still,
and takes hold of the bars,
and shakes them hard.

And she is all the time
trying to climb through.
But nobody could climb through
that pattern – it strangles so!

She gets through,
but then the pattern strangles her,
and turns her upside down,
and makes her eyes white.

# V

I think that woman
gets out in the daytime!
And I'll tell you why –
I've seen her!

I can see her out of the window.
It is the same woman.
I know it is the same woman,
because she is always creeping,
and most women
do not creep by daylight.

I see her creeping
all around the garden,
or on the road.
When someone comes, she hides.

I don't blame her.
You don't want to be caught
creeping by daylight.
I always lock the door
when I creep by daylight.
I can't do it at night
because John would suspect something.

**suspect** – think
something was
wrong

# VI

Hooray! This is the last day,
but it is enough.

John is staying in town tonight,
and won't be back till tomorrow.

As soon as it was moonlight,
and that poor thing began to creep
and shake the pattern,
I got up and ran to help her.

I pulled and she shook.
I shook and she pulled,
and before morning
we had pulled off yards of that paper.

And then when the sun came out
and that pattern began to laugh at me,
I declared I would finish it today!

**declared** –
said firmly

I must get to work!

I have locked the door,
and thrown the key down onto the path.

23

I don't want to go out,
and I don't want anybody to come in,
till John comes.

I want to surprise him.

But I forgot I could not reach far
without anything to stand on.

This bed will *not* move!

**lame** – unable
to move

I tried to lift and push it
until I was lame,
and then I got so angry
I bit off a little piece at one corner –
but it hurt my teeth.
I don't like to look out of the window –
there are so many of those
creeping women,
and they all creep so fast.

I wonder if they all
came out of the wallpaper as I did?

I suppose I will have to get back
behind the pattern at night,
and that will be hard.

It is so pleasant
to be out in this great room,
and creep around as I please.
I can creep smoothly on the floor,
and my shoulder just fits in
that long streak around the wall,
so I cannot lose my way.

Why, there's John at the door.

It is no use, young man.
You can't open it!

**pound** – bang on
the door

How he does call and pound!

Now he's crying out for an axe.
It would be a shame
to break down that beautiful door!

'John, dear!' I said
in the gentlest voice.
'The key is down on the path.'

That silenced him for a few moments.

Then he said, very quietly indeed,
'Open the door, my darling!'

'I can't,' I said.
'The key is down on the path!'
And then I said it again, several times,
very gently and very slowly,
and said it so often
that he had to go and see.

He got it of course,
and came in.

He stopped short by the door.

'What is the matter?' he cried.
'For God's sake, what are you doing?'

I kept on creeping just the same,
but I looked at him over my shoulder.

'I've got out at last,' I said,
'in spite of you.
And I've pulled off most of the paper,
so you can't put me back.'

Now why should that man
have fainted?

But he did,
and right across my path by the wall,
so that I have to creep over him
every time.